Exploring Tintagel Castle:
A Guide to Its History and Legends

EXPLORING TINTAGEL CASTLE

A Guide to Its History and Legends

Exploring Tintagel Castle

Exploring Tintagel Castle

TABLE OF CONTENTS

I Introduction	7
II Early History	11
III Medieval Period	15
IV The Tudor Era	19
V Modern History	23
VI The Castle Today	31
VII Legends and Folklore	36
VIII Archaeology	42
IX The Surrounding Area	46
X Planning Your Visit	50
XI Conclusion	54
XII Additional Resources	57

Exploring Tintagel Castle

Exploring Tintagel Castle

INTRODUCTION

An introduction to Tintagel Castle

Exploring Tintagel Castle

Nestled on the rugged coastline of Cornwall, Tintagel Castle stands as a testament to Britain's rich history and enduring legacy. The castle's ancient ruins and breathtaking views have captured the imaginations of visitors and locals alike for centuries, inspiring legends and folklore that continue to this day.

Tintagel Castle's history is as fascinating as it is complex, with evidence of occupation dating back to the Roman era. Over the centuries, the castle has been the site of battles, political intrigue, and royal connections, including its association with the legendary King Arthur.

In this ebook, we'll take a journey through time to explore the history, legends, and lore of Tintagel Castle.

Exploring Tintagel Castle

We'll delve into its early origins, examine its medieval and Tudor periods, and trace its modern-day transformation into a popular tourist attraction. Along the way, we'll explore the archaeology of the site, uncover the mysteries and myths that surround it, and offer practical tips for planning your own visit.

Whether you're a history buff, a fan of legends and folklore, or simply looking for a unique travel destination, Tintagel Castle is sure to captivate and inspire. So, come with us on a journey through time, and discover the wonder and magic of this remarkable site.

Exploring Tintagel Castle

Exploring Tintagel Castle

EARLY HISTORY

The beginnings of Tintagel Castle and the legend of King Arthur

Exploring Tintagel Castle

Tintagel Castle's history is shrouded in mystery, with much of its early origins still unknown. However, archaeological excavations have revealed evidence of occupation dating back to the Roman era, when the castle site may have been used as a trading post.

In the 5th and 6th centuries, Tintagel Castle was part of the kingdom of Dumnonia, which encompassed much of present-day Cornwall and Devon. During this time, the site may have served as a royal residence, with wealthy rulers commissioning the construction of grand buildings and fortifications.

Perhaps the most famous legend associated with Tintagel Castle is its connection to King Arthur, the legendary British king. According to the medieval writer Geoffrey of Monmouth, Tintagel was the birthplace of Arthur, conceived by his father Uther Pendragon and mother Ygraine, the wife of Duke

Exploring Tintagel Castle

Gorlois of Cornwall. However, this claim is not supported by any historical evidence and is likely a later invention.

Despite the lack of concrete evidence, the legend of King Arthur has captured the imaginations of generations, with many visitors to Tintagel Castle hoping to uncover clues to the king's mythical past. In recent years, archaeological excavations have uncovered evidence of high-status buildings at Tintagel during the 5th and 6th centuries, lending some credence to the idea that the site was a royal stronghold.

Regardless of the truth behind the King Arthur legend, Tintagel Castle's early history is a fascinating glimpse into Britain's ancient past. As we'll see in the following chapters, the castle would go on to play an important role in the country's history and cultural identity.

Exploring Tintagel Castle

Exploring Tintagel Castle

MEDIEVAL PERIOD

Tintagel Castle through the middle ages

Exploring Tintagel Castle

The medieval period of Tintagel Castle's history saw the site become an important strategic stronghold in Cornwall. In the 12th century, the castle was owned by Richard, Earl of Cornwall, who built a new great hall and other fortifications.

During this time, Tintagel Castle played a key role in the power struggles between the English and the Cornish. In 1233, the castle was besieged by Richard, Earl of Cornwall's own brother, King Henry III, who was attempting to assert his control over the region. The siege was ultimately unsuccessful, and the castle remained in the hands of the Earls of Cornwall.

Tintagel Castle's association with the legendary King Arthur continued to be a source of fascination during the medieval period, with stories of the king's exploits becoming more elaborate and fantastical. In the 15th century, the writer Thomas Malory included Tintagel in his seminal work, Le Morte

Exploring Tintagel Castle

d'Arthur, solidifying the castle's place in Arthurian legend.

Despite its important role in medieval history, Tintagel Castle gradually fell into disrepair in the centuries that followed. By the 16th century, the castle was abandoned, and its once-grand buildings and fortifications were left to crumble.

Today, visitors to Tintagel Castle can explore the medieval ruins and imagine the bustling activity and political intrigue that once took place within its walls. The castle's rich history and cultural significance continue to inspire and captivate, drawing visitors from around the world to this remarkable site.

Exploring Tintagel Castle

Exploring Tintagel Castle

THE TUDOR ERA

Tintagel Castle after the War of the Roses
and the very first tourists

Exploring Tintagel Castle

The Tudor era marked a time of great change and upheaval for Tintagel Castle. In the late 15th century, the Wars of the Roses had come to an end, and the victorious Tudor dynasty sought to consolidate their power by strengthening their hold on the south-west of England.

Tintagel Castle was one of many castles in the region that underwent significant changes during this time. The castle was owned by the Earls of Cornwall, who were closely allied with the Tudor monarchs. In 1487, the Earl of Cornwall, Henry Tudor (later King Henry VII), marched through Cornwall with an army to claim the throne from the Yorkist king, Richard III. Tintagel Castle likely played a strategic role in this campaign, providing a secure base of operations for Henry's troops.

Following his victory at the Battle of Bosworth Field, Henry Tudor became King Henry VII and embarked on a program of strengthening royal control over

Exploring Tintagel Castle

the country. Tintagel Castle was one of many castles that underwent significant renovation during this time, with new fortifications and buildings added to the site.

One of the most significant changes made to Tintagel Castle during the Tudor era was the construction of a new courtyard, or "Lower Ward," on the eastern side of the castle. This area was enclosed by a curtain wall, with two towers providing additional defense. The new courtyard likely served as a base for the castle's garrison, as well as providing storage and accommodation for troops and supplies.

The castle's association with King Arthur continued to be a source of fascination during the Tudor era, with the site becoming a popular destination for tourists and antiquarians. In 1534, the antiquarian John Leland visited Tintagel Castle and wrote about his experiences there. He noted the castle's

Exploring Tintagel Castle

connection to Arthurian legend, describing the site as "the very castle of the King Arthur of whom the Britons speak so much."

Despite the castle's renovations and continued cultural significance, Tintagel Castle gradually fell out of use as a military stronghold in the centuries that followed. By the 16th century, the castle was abandoned, and its once-grand buildings and fortifications were left to crumble.

Today, visitors to Tintagel Castle can explore the Tudor-era ruins and imagine the bustling activity and political intrigue that once took place within its walls.

Exploring Tintagel Castle

MODERN HISTORY

Modern history at Tintagel Castle and the tourist attraction

Exploring Tintagel Castle

The modern history of Tintagel Castle is closely tied to its role as a tourist attraction. Although the castle had fallen into disrepair by the 16th century, it continued to hold a special place in the cultural imagination of the British people. Throughout the 19th and early 20th centuries, Tintagel Castle became an increasingly popular destination for tourists and antiquarians, drawn by its connection to the legendary King Arthur.

In the mid-19th century, the castle was acquired by the Duchy of Cornwall, which undertook a series of renovations to make the site more accessible to visitors. These renovations included the construction of a new entrance and visitor center, as well as the stabilization and preservation of the castle's ruins. The castle was officially opened to the public in 1930, and it has remained a popular destination for tourists ever since.

Exploring Tintagel Castle

One of the most notable changes made to the castle in recent years was the construction of a new footbridge in 2019. The bridge spans the gap between the mainland and the island on which the castle is situated, providing a more secure and accessible route for visitors. The bridge was designed by the architectural firm Ney & Partners, and it has won multiple awards for its innovative design and engineering.

Another recent development at Tintagel Castle is the opening of a new visitor center in 2016. The center was built to replace the original visitor center, which had become outdated and cramped. The new center features modern facilities, including a café, gift shop, and interactive exhibits about the castle's history and cultural significance. The center also provides information about the castle's ongoing preservation efforts and the work being done to protect the site for future generations.

Exploring Tintagel Castle

Preserving the castle's ruins is an ongoing challenge, as the site is exposed to the elements and vulnerable to erosion and other forms of damage. In recent years, the English Heritage organization has undertaken a series of conservation efforts to protect the castle's ruins and ensure that they remain accessible to visitors. These efforts have included the installation of new drainage systems, the removal of vegetation that was damaging the site, and the stabilization of the castle's walls and foundations.

Despite the challenges of preserving a site as old and iconic as Tintagel Castle, the site continues to attract visitors from around the world. Its rich history, stunning location, and cultural significance make it a must-see destination for anyone interested in British history and folklore. Whether exploring the castle's medieval ruins,

Exploring Tintagel Castle

admiring the stunning views of the Cornish coastline, or simply enjoying a cup of tea in the visitor center, visitors to Tintagel Castle are sure to be captivated by its timeless beauty and enduring appeal.

Exploring Tintagel Castle

Exploring Tintagel Castle

THE CASTLE TODAY

Tintagel Castle today and ongoing preservation efforts

Exploring Tintagel Castle

Today, Tintagel Castle is a popular tourist destination that attracts visitors from all over the world. The castle's stunning location on the Cornish coast, its rich history and cultural significance, and its ongoing preservation efforts make it a must-see destination for anyone interested in British history and folklore.

Visitors to Tintagel Castle can expect to see a range of impressive features, from the ruins of the medieval castle to the stunning views of the surrounding coastline. The castle's ruins include the remains of the Great Hall, the chapel, and the outer walls, among other features. Visitors can explore the castle's many nooks and crannies, imagining what life would have been like for the people who lived and worked there centuries ago.

Exploring Tintagel Castle

In addition to the castle ruins, visitors can also enjoy a range of other features at Tintagel Castle. The castle's visitor center provides a wealth of information about the castle's history and cultural significance, as well as the ongoing preservation efforts that are being undertaken to protect the site. The center also features a café and gift shop, making it a great place to grab a bite to eat or pick up a souvenir.

One of the most impressive features of Tintagel Castle is its location. The castle is perched on a rocky outcropping that overlooks the sea, providing stunning views of the Cornish coastline. Visitors can take a leisurely stroll along the castle's many paths and walkways, soaking in the beauty of the surrounding landscape.

Exploring Tintagel Castle

Preserving the castle's ruins is an ongoing challenge, but a range of efforts are underway to ensure that the site remains accessible and safe for visitors. These efforts include ongoing conservation work to stabilize the castle's walls and foundations, as well as the installation of new drainage systems and other infrastructure improvements.

One of the most significant preservation efforts currently underway at Tintagel Castle is the construction of a new walkway that will provide visitors with improved access to the castle's ruins. The walkway, which is expected to be completed in 2023, will allow visitors to explore parts of the castle that were previously inaccessible, providing a more immersive and engaging experience.

Exploring Tintagel Castle

Another important preservation effort at Tintagel Castle is the removal of invasive plant species that have been damaging the castle's ruins. In recent years, English Heritage has undertaken a series of projects to remove these species and restore the castle's natural environment. These efforts are critical to protecting the castle's ruins and ensuring that they remain accessible to visitors for years to come.

In conclusion, Tintagel Castle remains a fascinating and engaging destination for visitors from around the world. Its rich history, stunning location, and ongoing preservation efforts make it a must-see destination for anyone interested in British history and folklore. From exploring the castle's ruins to admiring the stunning views of the Cornish coastline, visitors to Tintagel Castle are sure to be captivated by its timeless beauty and enduring appeal.

Exploring Tintagel Castle

LEGENDS AND FOLKLORE

The legends and myths of Tintagel Castle

Exploring Tintagel Castle

Tintagel Castle is steeped in myths, legends, and folklore, many of which have been passed down through the ages. Perhaps the most famous legend associated with Tintagel Castle is the story of King Arthur, who is said to have been conceived at the site. But this is just one of many legends and tales that are associated with this historic site.

According to legend, Tintagel Castle was the birthplace of King Arthur, the legendary warrior king who led the Knights of the Round Table. The story goes that Arthur's father, Uther Pendragon, fell in love with Igraine, the wife of the Duke of Cornwall, and used magic to disguise himself as her husband. Igraine became pregnant as a result of this deception, and she gave birth to Arthur at Tintagel Castle.

Exploring Tintagel Castle

The legend of King Arthur has captured the imagination of people for centuries, and Tintagel Castle has become a pilgrimage site for Arthurian enthusiasts from around the world. The castle ruins, with their dramatic setting on the Cornish coast, seem to embody the spirit of Arthurian legend, making Tintagel Castle an especially powerful symbol of Britain's ancient past.

In addition to the story of King Arthur, there are many other myths and legends associated with Tintagel Castle. One popular legend is that of Tristan and Isolde, a tragic love story that has been told and retold in various forms throughout the ages.

Exploring Tintagel Castle

According to the legend, Tristan was a knight who fell in love with Isolde, the beautiful wife of his uncle, King Mark. The two of them began a secret affair, but their love was ultimately doomed, and they both met tragic ends. Tintagel Castle is said to have been the site of their first meeting, adding another layer of romance and intrigue to the castle's already rich history.

Other legends associated with Tintagel Castle include stories of mermaids and sea monsters, tales of ghosts and haunted chambers, and stories of heroic knights and valiant battles. Many of these legends have been passed down through the ages, with each generation adding its own unique twist to the tales.

Exploring Tintagel Castle

The legends and folklore associated with Tintagel Castle have helped to cement its place in the popular imagination. They have also helped to inspire countless works of literature, art, and music over the centuries, from the epic poetry of the medieval era to the modern-day blockbuster movies that continue to captivate audiences around the world.

For visitors to Tintagel Castle, the legends and folklore associated with the site can add an extra layer of meaning and depth to their experience. By exploring the castle's ruins and contemplating its rich history, visitors can begin to appreciate the enduring power of myth and legend in shaping our understanding of the past.

Exploring Tintagel Castle

In conclusion, the legends and folklore associated with Tintagel Castle are an integral part of its history and cultural significance. From the legend of King Arthur to the tales of Tristan and Isolde and beyond, the stories associated with this historic site have captivated the imaginations of people for centuries. By exploring these myths and legends, visitors to Tintagel Castle can gain a deeper appreciation of its enduring appeal and the role it continues to play in shaping our understanding of Britain's ancient past.

Exploring Tintagel Castle

ARCHAEOLOGY

The ruins and findings at Tintagel Castle and its surroundings

Exploring Tintagel Castle

Tintagel Castle has a rich archaeological history that has helped to uncover many of the secrets of its past. From excavations carried out in the 1930s to more recent investigations, the site has revealed numerous artifacts and structures that provide insight into its use and development over the centuries.

One of the most significant archaeological finds at Tintagel was made in the 1930s by archaeologist Ralegh Radford. He uncovered a series of slate-lined storage pits that were used for the storage of food and other supplies. These pits have been dated to the 5th and 6th centuries, providing evidence that the site was occupied during the period that has been associated with King Arthur.

Exploring Tintagel Castle

More recent excavations have also uncovered evidence of a large-scale metalworking operation at Tintagel. A team of archaeologists led by English Heritage and Cornwall Archaeological Unit carried out excavations in the 1990s, uncovering a wealth of artifacts and structures that provide insight into the industrial activity that took place at the site during the medieval period.

Among the finds were the remains of a smelting furnace, which would have been used to extract metal from its ores. The furnace was constructed using local slate, and its remains have been carefully preserved so that visitors can see the impressive engineering skill that went into its construction.

Exploring Tintagel Castle

Other artifacts uncovered during the excavations include crucibles, molds, and slag, providing evidence of the various processes involved in metalworking. The finds indicate that the site was a major center for the production of high-quality metal objects during the medieval period, and that it played an important role in the economy of the region.

The archaeological finds at Tintagel continue to provide new insights into the site's history, and ongoing excavations and research are likely to reveal even more about its past. Visitors to the site can see some of the artifacts and structures uncovered during excavations in the on-site exhibition, providing a fascinating glimpse into the history of this remarkable place.

Exploring Tintagel Castle

SURROUNDING AREA

The surroundings of Tintagel Castle and the Cornish coast

Exploring Tintagel Castle

Tintagel Castle is situated in an area of outstanding natural beauty, and there are many other historical sites and attractions nearby that visitors can explore.

One of the most popular nearby attractions is the Arthurian Centre, which is dedicated to the legends and folklore surrounding King Arthur and the Knights of the Round Table. The center features exhibits and interactive displays that provide insight into the stories and characters that have become synonymous with Tintagel and the surrounding area.

Another nearby attraction is the St Nectan's Glen Waterfall, which is a stunning natural feature that has been attracting visitors for centuries. The waterfall is situated in a wooded valley and is surrounded by ancient trees and steep cliffs, providing a tranquil and peaceful setting that is perfect for a relaxing walk.

Exploring Tintagel Castle

For those interested in exploring more of the region's history, the nearby town of Boscastle is well worth a visit. The town is home to the Museum of Witchcraft and Magic, which is dedicated to the history of witchcraft and the occult in the UK. The museum features exhibits and artifacts that provide a fascinating insight into this dark and mysterious aspect of the country's history.

Other nearby historical sites include the medieval castle ruins at Launceston and the picturesque fishing village of Port Isaac, which is famous for its narrow streets and stunning views of the coastline. Overall, the surrounding area of Tintagel Castle is rich in history and natural beauty, providing a wealth of attractions and activities that are sure to delight visitors of all ages.

Exploring Tintagel Castle

Exploring Tintagel Castle

PLANNING YOUR VISIT

Plan your visit to Tintagel Castle

Exploring Tintagel Castle

Tintagel Castle is a popular tourist destination, attracting visitors from all over the world who come to marvel at its stunning coastal location and rich history. If you're planning a visit to Tintagel Castle, here are some practical tips and information to help you make the most of your experience.

Getting There

Tintagel Castle is located on the North Cornwall coast, about 40 miles west of Plymouth and 25 miles north of Newquay. The nearest major airport is Newquay Airport, which has regular flights from various UK cities.

If you're driving, the castle is easily accessible via the A39, which runs from Bath to Falmouth. There is limited parking available at the castle, and it can get quite busy during peak season, so it's best to arrive early if you're driving.

Exploring Tintagel Castle

Alternatively, you can take public transportation. The nearest train station is Bodmin Parkway, which is about 20 miles away. From there, you can take a bus or taxi to Tintagel.

Opening Hours and Admission

Tintagel Castle is open daily from 10am to 4pm. Admission prices vary depending on the time of year, with discounts available for children, seniors, and students.

It's a good idea to book your tickets in advance, particularly during peak season when the castle can get very busy. You can book online via the English Heritage website.

Exploring Tintagel Castle

What to Expect

Tintagel Castle is an outdoor attraction, so it's important to dress appropriately for the weather. The castle is located on a steep hill, so wear comfortable shoes and be prepared for some uphill walking.

There are plenty of information boards and signage throughout the castle, so it's easy to navigate and learn about the history of the site. There are also audio guides available for an additional fee.

There are several cafes and gift shops on site, as well as toilets and baby changing facilities. The castle is wheelchair accessible, although some parts of the site may be challenging for those with mobility issues.

Exploring Tintagel Castle

CONCLUSION

Tintagel Castle through the ages

Exploring Tintagel Castle

Tintagel Castle is a truly unique and fascinating historical site, with a rich and varied history that spans thousands of years. From its early origins as a Celtic fortress to its role in the Arthurian legends, and from its medieval heyday to its current status as a popular tourist attraction, Tintagel Castle has captured the imaginations of people for centuries.

Throughout this ebook, we have explored the many facets of Tintagel Castle's history, from its legends and folklore to its archaeological discoveries and ongoing preservation efforts. We have seen how the castle has played a key role in shaping the history of Cornwall and the wider UK, and how it continues to inspire and delight visitors from all over the world.

Exploring Tintagel Castle

As we conclude our journey through the history of Tintagel Castle, we can reflect on the enduring legacy of this remarkable site. Its stories and legends continue to capture our imaginations, and its rich history offers us a glimpse into the lives of those who came before us.

Whether you are a history buff, an archaeology enthusiast, or simply someone who appreciates the beauty of nature and the power of myth, Tintagel Castle is a must-see destination that is sure to leave a lasting impression. We hope that this ebook has inspired you to visit Tintagel Castle and discover its magic for yourself.

Exploring Tintagel Castle

ADDITIONAL RESOURCES

Read more about Tintagel Castle and the legend of King Arthur

Exploring Tintagel Castle

1. <u>Tintagel Castle Official Website</u>: The official website for Tintagel Castle provides information on opening hours, admission prices, and upcoming events, as well as historical information and visitor guides.

2. <u>English Heritage</u>: English Heritage is the organization that manages and cares for Tintagel Castle. Their website provides additional historical and archaeological information, as well as resources for educators and researchers.

3. <u>Visit Cornwall</u>: Visit Cornwall is the official tourism website for the county of Cornwall, where Tintagel Castle is located. Their website provides information on other nearby attractions, accommodations, and travel information.

Exploring Tintagel Castle

4. <u>The King Arthur Trail</u>: The King Arthur Trail is a walking route that takes visitors through the historic sites associated with the legend of King Arthur, including Tintagel Castle. The trail is well-signposted and offers stunning views of the Cornish coastline.

5. <u>The Arthurian Society</u>: The Arthurian Society is a scholarly organization dedicated to the study of Arthurian legend and its cultural significance. Their website provides a wealth of resources for researchers and enthusiasts, including a bibliography of Arthurian studies and links to related organizations.

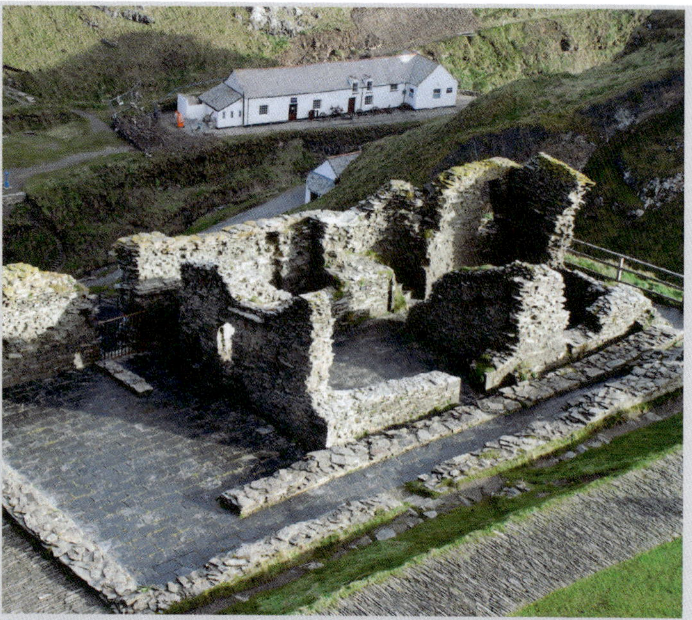

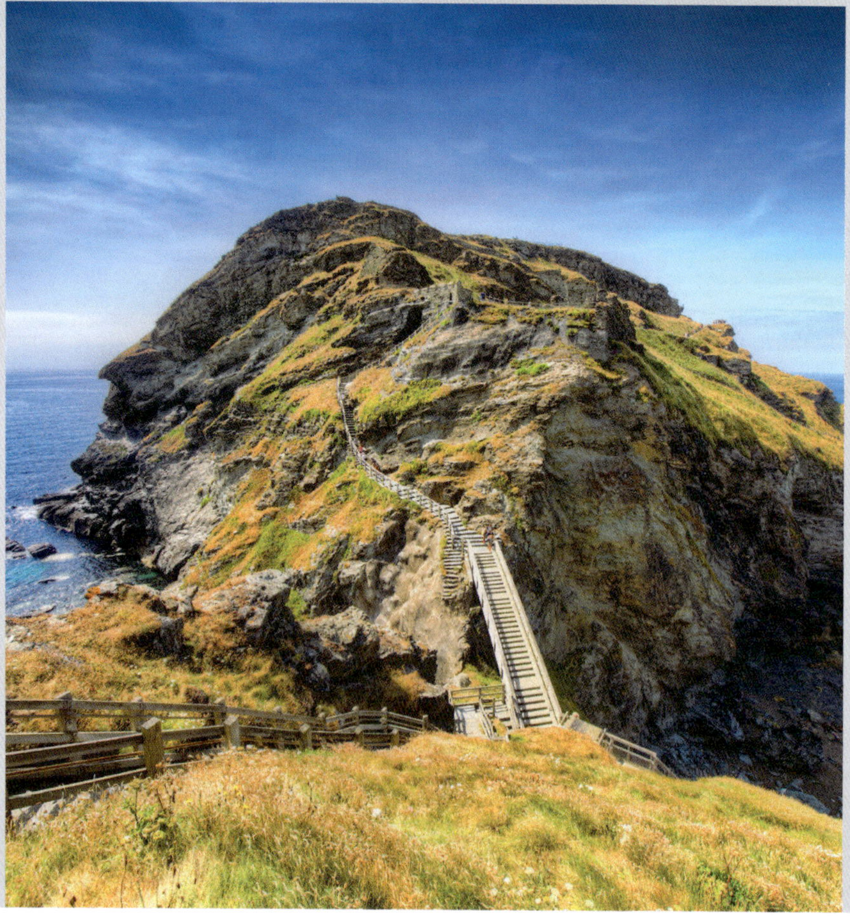

Printed in Great Britain
by Amazon